Mortals and Angels:

A Bluegrass TE DEUM

Libretto by: Marisha Chamberlain
Music by: Carol Barnett

Full Score and Set of Parts for Bluegrass Band #48024278

ISBN: 1540041824

BOOSEY & HAWKES

DISTRIBUTED BY
HAL•LEONARD®

Visit Hal Leonard Online at
www.halleonard.com

CAST OF CHARACTERS

The Mortals: A Bluegrass band

The Angels: Adult choir, possibly in various shades of white and cream and light gray, not uniform but offering the suggestion that angels are individuals

The Archangel: a baritone soloist from the choir

The Kids: Treble choir

The Conductor: dressed either in standard concert wear (preferable) or in the same style as the Bluegrass band—No "Heehaw" costumes.

"In any age, life has to be lived before we can know what it is."
Lisel Mueller,
"The Triumph of Life"

PROGRAM NOTE

Commissioned by the *Distinguished Concerts International New York (DCINY) Premiere Project* and premiered at Carnegie Hall in January 2016 with the *DCINY Singers International* and award-winning Nashville bluegrass band *Dailey and Vincent*, **Mortals & Angels: A Bluegrass TE DEUM** is now available in this revised version.

The **Te Deum** is a Latin prayer that many composers have set to music. But never before has there been a **Te Deum** for chorus and Bluegrass band. In Latin, **Te Deum Laudamus** means "Thee, O God we praise", and in the first words of the prayer, all creation praises God. Mortals and Angels praise God. There's something about angels; the ancient idea of winged messengers occurs in almost every religion. Representations of angels in art tend to be human shapes with wings added, and in many traditions, angels willingly guide us. We mortals, however, have problems with guidance. How on earth would angels know better what we should or should not do, given their immortality and their ability to hover, appear and disappear? We will eventually die, while they fly on and on. In this setting the Angels are represented by the choir, the Mortals by the band. And there are the kids—sometimes Angels, sometimes very mortal. And out in the audience: Mortals? or Angels?

Dedicated to Distinguished Concerts International New York and our Soaring Dreams Supporters

MORTALS AND ANGELS: A BLUEGRASS TE DEUM

I. Angel of God

SATB Choir, Gospel Quartet and Keyboard with Optional Instrumental Accompaniment*

Marisha Chamberlain
adapted from a traditional prayer

Carol Barnett

* Score and parts for fiddle, mandolin, banjo, guitar and bass are available as a digital download from the publisher at halleonard.com (#48024278)

979-0-051-48498-0

Engraved & Printed in U.S.A.

9
S.
A.
pp
Mm
T.
B.
T. I
G.Q.
T. II
Ev - er this day Be at my side To light and guard And rule and guide.
Kbd.
13
S.
A.
T.
B.
T. I
G.Q.
An-gel of God, My guard - ian dear, To whom God's love En - trusts me here,
mp
T. II
An-gel of God, My guard - ian dear, To whom God's love En - trusts me here,
G Em D G Em G C G Em D
Kbd.
+ Banjo & Bass

17
S.
A.
Oo
pp
T.
B.
T. I
Ev - er this day Be at my side To light and guard And rule and guide.
G.Q.
T. II
Ev - er this day Be at my side To light and guard And rule and guide.
C D Em C Em Am Em
Kbd.
21
S.
A.
mf
3
Ev - er this day We're at your side To
T.
B.
mf
3
T. I
A - men.
G.Q.
T. II
A - men.
Em C Em C Em C
Kbd.

25
S.
A.
mp
light and guard And rule and guide. A -
T.
B.
mp
T. I
G.Q.
T. II
Kbd.
28
p
men. A - men.
p
T. I
G.Q.
T. II
Kbd.

II. Te Deum

SATB Choir, Gospel Quartet, Treble Chorus and Keyboard

Traditional / Marisha Chamberlain

Carol Barnett

Con spirito ♩. = ca. 76
Soprano
Alto
Tenor
Bass
mf
Te De - um_ lau - da - mus_ Te
Con spirito ♩. = ca. 76
Fiddle, Mandolin, Banjo, Guitar, Bass
A
Amaj7
Piano
mf
5
S.
Do - mi-num con - fi - te - mur._ Lau - da - mus Te, lau - da - mus Te, Te
A.
mf
Lau - da - mus Te, lau - da - mus Te, Te
T.
mf
Lau - da - mus Te, lau - da - mus Te, Te
B.
mf
Lau - da - mus Te, lau - da - mus Te, Te
D
C♯m
Kbd.

979-0-051-48498-0

Engraved & Printed in U.S.A.

9
S.
Do - mi - num_ con - fi - te - mur._
A.
Do - mi - num_ con - fi - te - mur._
T.
Do - mi - num_ con - fi - te - mur._ Te - De - um_ lau - da - mus_ Te
B.
Do - mi - num_ con - fi - te - mur._ Te - De - um_ lau - da - mus_ Te
A
Amaj7
Kbd.
13
S.
Lau - da - mus te, lau - de - mus te, Te
A.
Lau - da - mus te, lau - de - mus te, Te
T.
Do - mi-num con - fi - te - mur._ Lau - da - mus te, lau - de - mus te, Te
B.
Do - mi-num con - fi - te - mur._ Lau - da - mus te, lau - de - mus te, Te
D
A
Kbd.

17
S.
A.
T.
B.
Kbd.
p
Do - mi - num_ con - fi - te - mur._ Te ae - ter - nam Pa - trem_ Om - nis
C♯m
E/G♯
21
ter - ra ve - ne - ra - tur. Ti - bi_ om - nes An - ge - li;_
ter - ra ve - ne - ra - tur. Ti - bi om - nes An - ge - li;
C♯m
G♯m
G
A/G
G

25
S.
A.
T.
B.
Kbd.
cresc.
mf
Ti - bi cae - li et u - ni - ver - sae Po - tes - ta - tes;
A/G G A/G G C/G Fmaj7
28
p leggiero
Ti - bi, Ti - bi Cher - u - bim et Ser - a - phim
Ti - bi Cher - u - bim et Ser - a - phim In - ces -
Ti - bi,
E
p

31
S.
A.
T.
B.
Kbd.
cresc. poco a poco
In - ces - sa - bi - li, In - ces - sa - bi - li, In - ce - sa - bi - li,
sa - bi - li, In - ces - sa - bi - li, In - ces - sa - bi - li, In - ces -
p leggiero
In - ces - sa - bi - li, In - ces - sa - bi - li, In - ces -
34
In - ce - sa - bi - li vo - ce pro - cla - mant:
sa - bi - li, In - ces - sa - bi - li vo - ce pro - cla - mant:
sa - bi - li, In - ces - sa - bi - li vo - ce, vo - ce pro - cla - mant:
mf cresc.
vo - ce pro - cla - mant:
Am7/G
Dm/F

979-0-051-48498-0

979-0-051-48498-0

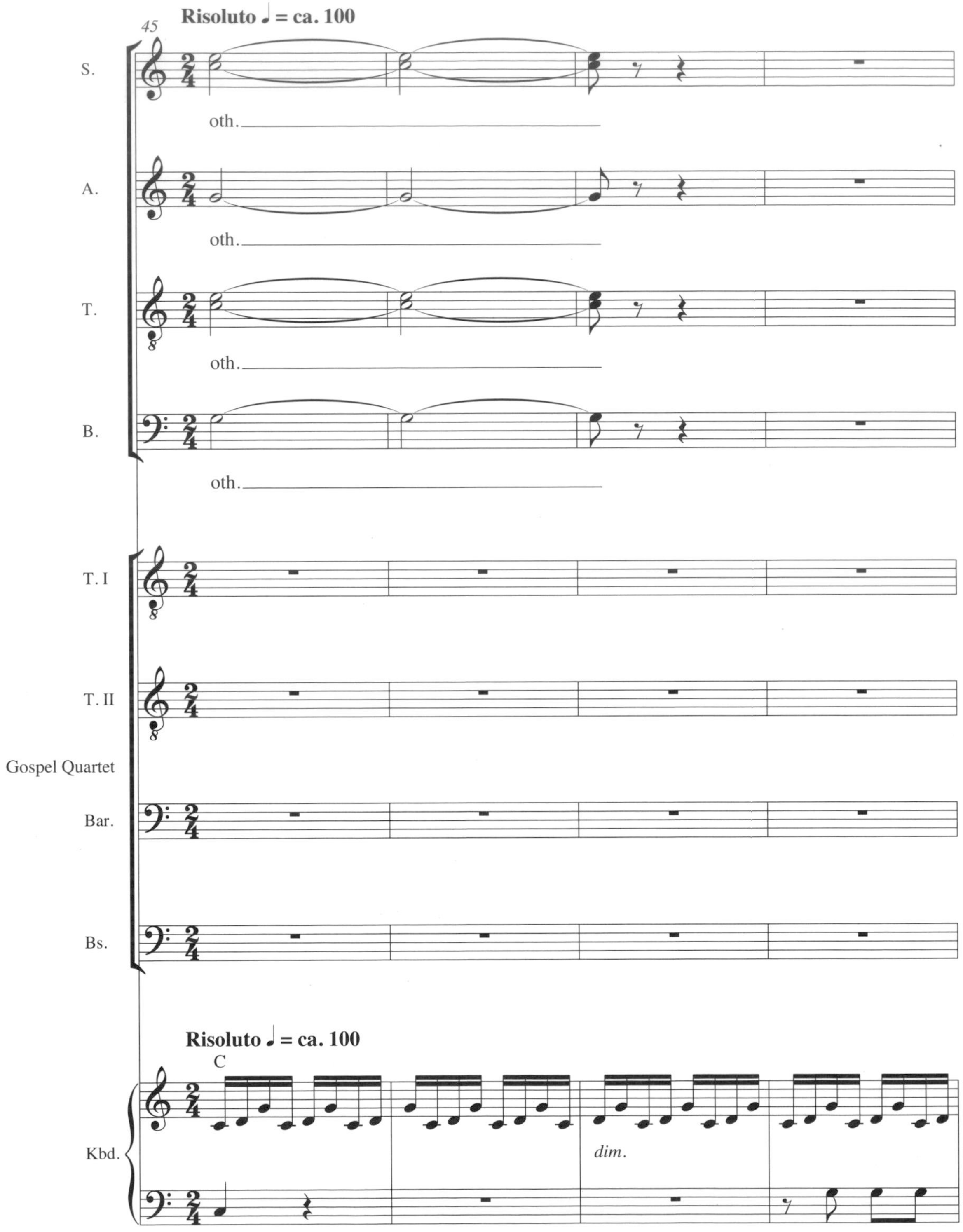
45
Risoluto ♩ = ca. 100
S.
oth.
A.
oth.
T.
oth.
B.
oth.
T. I
T. II
Gospel Quartet
Bar.
Bs.
Risoluto ♩ = ca. 100
C
Kbd.
dim.

49
S.
A.
T.
B.
mf
T. I
All of earth a-dores Thee, Lord God a - bove, All of earth a-dores Thee,
T. II
mf
Lord God a - bove,
G.Q.
Bar.
mf
Lord God a - bove,
Bs.
mf
Lord God a - bove,
Kbd.
mf

55
S.
A.
T.
B.
mf
et An - ge-li, et An - ge-li,
T. I
T. II
G.Q.
Bar.
Bs.
Lord God a - bove. Mor- tals, Mor- tals,
Kbd.
F C F Em

61
S.
A.
T.
B.
T. I
p
we a - dore Thee, we a - dore Thee, we a - dore Thee, we a - dore Thee, we a - dore Thee,
T. II
p
we a - dore Thee, we a - dore Thee, we a - dore Thee,
G.Q.
Bar.
p
we a - dore Thee,
Bs.
Kbd.
C
p

66
S.
A.
T.
B.
T. I
cresc.
mf
we a-dore Thee, we a - dore.__ All__ of earth a-dores Thee, Lord God a - bove,
T. II
cresc.
mf
we a-dore Thee, we a-dore Thee, Lord. Lord God a - bove,
G.Q.
Bar.
cresc.
mf
we a-dore Thee, we a-dore Thee, Lord. Lord God a - bove,
Bs.
cresc.
mf
we a-dore Thee, we a-dore Thee, Lord. Lord God a - bove, O Lord- y,
G C
Kbd.
cresc.
mf

72
S.
A.
T.
B.
mf
et An - ge - li,
T. I
T. II
G.Q.
Bar.
Bs.
Lord God a - bove. Mor - tals,
All__ of earth a - dores Thee, Lord God a - bove. Mor - tals,
O. Lord God a - bove, O Lord - y. Mor - tals,
F
C
Kbd.

78
S.
Treble Chorus
A.
mp
Fa-thers, moth-ers,
Fa - thers, moth-ers,
S.
A.
T.
B.
et Cher - u-bim et Ser - a - phim,
sub. p
cae - li et u - ni-ver-sae
T. I
T. II
Gospel Quartet
Bar.
Bs.
Mor- tals,
F Em Dm Em Dm C
Kbd.
sub. p

83
S.
T.C.
A.
chil-dren, Un-cles, aunts and cous - ins, Fa-thers, moth-ers,
chil-dren, Un-cles, aunts and cous-ins, Fa-thers, moth-ers,
S.
A.
T.
B.
p
cae - li et u - ni-ver-sae
Po - tes-ta-tes; cae - li et u - ni-ver-sae Po-tes - ta - tes; cae - li et u - ni-ver-sae
T. I
T. II
G.Q.
Bar.
Bs.
Kbd.

979-0-051-48498-0

89
cresc. poco a poco
S.
T.C.
chil-dren, Un-cles, aunts and cous - ins, Fa - thers, moth - ers,
A.
chil-dren, Un-cles, aunts and cous-ins, Fa - thers, moth - ers,
S.
A.
mp cresc. poco a poco
cae - li et u - ni-ver-sae
T.
Po-tes-ta-tes; cae - li et u - ni-ver-sae Po-tes-ta-tes; cae - li et u - ni-ver-sae
B.
Po-tes-ta-tes; cae - li et u - ni-ver-sae Po-tes-ta-tes; cae - li et u - ni-ver-sae
T. I
T. II
G.Q.
Bar.
Bs.
Am
Em
Kbd.

979-0-051-48498-0

95
S.
T.C.
A.
chil-dren, Un-cles, aunts and cous-ins,
chil-dren, Un-cles, aunts and cous-ins,
S.
A.
T.
B.
Po-tes-ta-tes; cae - li et u - ni-ver-sae Po-tes-ta-tes;
Po-tes-ta-tes; cae - li et u - ni-ver-sae Po-tes-ta-tes;
Po-tes-ta-tes; cae - li et u - ni-ver-sae Po-tes-ta-tes; cae - li
T. I
T. II
G.Q.
Bar.
Bs.
All of
All of
All of
Em/G
C
Kbd.
f
mp

100
S.
T.C.
A.
f
Fa- thers, moth- ers, chil- dren, Un- cles, aunts and cous- ins,
f
Fa- thers, moth- ers, chil- dren, Un- cles, aunts and cous- ins,
S.
A.
T.
B.
et u - ni - ver - sae Po - tes - ta - tes;
T. I
mp
earth a-dores Thee, Lord God a - bove.
T. II
mp
earth a-dores Thee, Lord God a - bove.
G.Q.
Bar.
mp
earth a-dores Thee, Lord God a - bove.
Bs.
f
mp
Lord God a - bove.
C
Kbd.
mf

105
S.
T.C.
A.
f
Fa-thers, moth-ers, chil-dren, Un-cles,
f
Fa-thers, moth-ers, chil-dren, Un-cles,
S.
A.
T.
mp
cac - li et u - ni - ver - sae Po - tes -
B.
T. I
T. II
G.Q.
Bar.
Bs.
f
mp
Lord God a - bove.
Lord God a - bove.
Lord God a - bove.
All God's earth a-dores Thee, Lord God a - bove.
Kbd.
C
mf

110
S.
T.C.
A.
aunts and cous - ins,
a - dore Thee,
aunts and cous - ins,
a - dore Thee,
S.
A.
T.
B.
f
ta - tes;
et An - ge - li,
et
T. I
T. II
G.Q.
Bar.
Bs.
Mor - tals,
Mor - tals,
F
C
F
Kbd.

115
cresc.
S.
T.C.
A.
a - dore Thee, a - dore Thee, a - dore Thee, a - dore Thy cre -
An - ge - li, a - dore Thee, a - dore Thee, a - dore Thy cre -
T.
B.
T. I
T. II
G.Q.
Bar.
Bs.
C
Kbd.

Poco meno mosso ♩ = ca. 96
120
S.
T.C.
A.
ff
a - tion.
mf
Te
S.
A.
T.
B.
T. I
T. II
G.Q.
Bar.
Bs.
Poco meno mosso ♩ = ca. 96
Kbd.
Banjo

125
S.
T.C.
A.
De - um lau - da - mus, lau - da-mus Te.
De - um lau - da - mus, lau - da-mus Te.
S.
A.
T.
B.
mf
p
Sanc - tus,
Sanc - tus,
Sanc - tus, Sanc - tus,
Sanc - tus, Sanc - tus,
T. I
T. II
G.Q.
Bar.
Bs.
Kbd.
A
E
A F♯m
E
A
mp

131
S.
T.C.
A.
Te De - um lau - da - mus, lau - da - mus Te.
Te De - um lau - da - mus, lau - da - mus Te.
S.
A.
T.
Sanc-tus Do-mi-nus De-us Sa - ba - oth.
B.
Sanc-tus Do-mi-nus De-us Sa - ba - oth.
T. I
T. II
G.Q.
Bar.
Bs.
E A E A F♯m E
Kbd.

979-0-051-48498-0

142
S.
T.C.
A.
da - mus, lau - da-mus Te.
Te De - um lau - da - mus, lau-
da - mus, lau - da-mus Te.
Te De - um lau - da - mus, lau-
S.
A.
T.
B.
mf
p
Sanc - tus, Sanc - tus,
Te De - um lau - da - mus, lau-
T. I
T. II
G.Q.
Bar.
Bs.
Kbd.
C♯
F♯
F♯
C♯

979-0-051-48498-0

153
S.
T.C.
A.
mf
a - dores Thee,_ a - dores Thy cre - a - tion,
a - dores Thee,_ a - dores Thy cre - a - tion,
S.
A.
T.
B.
oth.
Sanc - tus,
T. I
T. II
G.Q.
Bar.
Bs.
All_ of earth a-dores Thee, Lord God a - bove.
Lord God a - bove.
D A D A
Kbd.

159
S.
T.C.
A.
a - dores Thee, a - dores Thy cre - a - tion,
a - dores Thee, a - dores Thy cre - a - tion,
sub. p
mf
ah,
Sanc - tus,
ah,
Sanc - tus,
T.
ah,
Sanc - tus,
B.
ah,
Sanc - tus,
T. I
All of earth a-dores Thee, Lord God a - bove.
T. II
G.Q.
Lord God a - bove.
Bar.
Lord God a - bove.
Bs.
Lord God a - bove.
D
A
D
A
Kbd.

165
S.
T.C.
A.
p
a - dores Thy cre - a - tion,
mp
a -
S.
A.
T.
B.
sub. p
ah
mp
ah
T. I
T. II
G.Q.
Bar.
Bs.
p
All of earth a - dores Thee,
mp
all of earth a - dores Thee,
A
Kbd.
sub. p
mp

170
S.
T.C.
A.
mf
dores Thy cre - a - tion, lau - da - mus Te.
dores Thy cre - a - tion, lau - da - mus Te.
cresc. poco a poco
Sanc - tus, Sanc - tus, Sanc - tus, Sanc - tus,
T.
B.
T. I
T. II
G.Q.
Bar.
Bs.
all of earth a - dores Thee, all
C
A
Kbd.

979-0-051-48498-0

175
S.
T.C.
A.
cresc.
f
ff
All of earth a - dores Thee.
All of earth a - dores Thee.
S.
A.
Sanc - tus, Sanc - tus, Sanc - tus.
Sanc - tus, Sanc - tus, Sanc - tus.
T.
B.
Sanc - tus, Sanc - tus, Do - mi-nus De - us Sa - ba - oth.
Sanc - tus, Sanc - tus, Do - mi-nus De - us Sa - ba - oth.
T. I
T. II
G.Q.
Bar.
Bs.
of earth a - dores Thee.
of earth a - dores Thee.
of earth a - dores Thee.
of earth a - dores Thee.
Kbd.
B C C/G A

(Angels give each other 'high fives', expressing dominion over the Mortals.)

III. Who Makes the Sun to Rise?

Gospel Quartet and Band

Marisha Chamberlain

Carol Barnett

979-0-051-48498-0

Engraved & Printed in U.S.A.

11
T. I
me.
T. II
me.
Bar.
me.
Bs.
Who makes the sun to rise, the rain to fall, Who
D
G
Banjo
Guitar
Pno.
15
T. I
It ain't me, oh Lord, it ain't
T. II
It ain't me, oh Lord, it ain't
Bar.
It ain't me, oh Lord, it ain't
Bs.
turns the chill-y win-ter to spring? It ain't me, oh Lord, it ain't
C7
C6
G/D
D7
Pno.

20
T. I
me.
Who makes the sun to rise?
T. II
me.
It ain't me.
Bar.
me.
It ain't me.
Bs.
me.
It ain't me, it ain't
Pno.
G
C Am G
25
T. I
It ain't me.
Who makes the
T. II
Who makes the rain to fall?
It ain't me.
Bar.
It ain't me, it ain't me.
Bs.
me.
It ain't me, it ain't me.
Pno.
A7
D7

30
T. I
sun to rise, the rain to fall, Who?
T. II
Who?
Bar.
Who?
Bs.
Who turns the chill-y win-ter to spring?
G
G7
C7
Pno.
34
T. I
Well, it ain't me, oh Lord, it ain't me.
T. II
Well, it ain't me, oh Lord, it ain't me.
Bar.
Well, it ain't me, oh Lord, it ain't me.
Bs.
Well, it ain't me, oh Lord, it ain't me.
C6
G/D
D7
G
Pno.

40
T. I
T. II
Bar.
Bs.
Pno.
G
B♭
G
A7
D7
Am7
D7
(band improv.)
48
T. I
T. II
Bar.
Bs.
Pno.
G
C7
G/D
D7
G

56
T. I
T. II
Bar.
Bs.
G F G Bb G F D F D
Pno.
f
61
mf
Can you make the sun to rise?
mf
Nor can we.
Can you make the
mf
Nor can we.
mf
Nor can we.
C Am G
mf

66
T. I
T. II
Bar.
Bs.
Pno.
Nor can we. Can you make the sun to rise,
rain to fall? Nor can we. the
Nor can we.
Nor can we.
C/D D G
71
Can you turn the chill-y win-ter to spring?
rain to fall? Can you turn the chill-y win-ter to spring?
C C7

75
T. I
Nor can we, oh Lord, a-nor can we, oh Lord.
T. II
Nor can we, oh Lord, a-nor can we, oh Lord.
Bar.
Nor can we, oh Lord, a-nor can we, oh Lord.
Bs.
Nor can we, oh Lord, a-nor can we, oh Lord.
G/D D7 Em A7
Pno.
81
T. I
cresc. f
Nor can we, oh Lord.
T. II
cresc. f
Nor can we, oh Lord.
Bar.
cresc. f
Nor can we, oh Lord.
Bs.
cresc. f
Nor can we, oh Lord.
G/D C G
Pno.
cresc. f

(Mortals indicate that they have engaged in the contest with the Angels by giving each other 'high fives'. Angels indicate agreement in a condescending manner by giving tepid applause.)

IV. Holier Than Thou

Gospel Quartet and Band

Marisha Chamberlain

Carol Barnett

979-0-051-48498-0

Engraved & Printed in U.S.A.

19
T. I
T. II
Bar.
Bs.
Pno.
tutti mf
Then drop that an - gel at - ti - tude,
at - ti - tude, Ho-li - er than thou. Then drop that an - gel at - ti - tude,
C D G
24
Ho-li - er than thou.
Ho-li - er than thou.
G7 F/A Aaug D G D Bm
f
30
C A D Bm G7 F♯m/A G/B D Em7

37
T. I
T. II
Bar.
Bs.
Pno.
mf
You got that an - gel at - ti-tude,
Ho-li - er than
Dm/F C/E D Em7 D G7 Am7 D7
43
You got that an - gel at ti - tude, Make
thou. You got that an - gel at - ti - tude, Ho - li - er than thou, oh yeah!
thou. Ho - li - er than thou, oh yeah!
G7 Am7 D7

48
T. I
your-selves un - pop - u - lar with that an - gel at - ti - tude. Ho - li - er than
T. II
mp
Ah
mf
Ho - li - er than
Bar.
mp
Ah
mf
Ho - li - er than
Bs.
mp
Ah
mf
Ho - li - er than
G7 Dm7 G7 Dm7 G A
Pno.

53
T. I
thou, huh! Ho - li - er than thou!
T. II
thou, huh! Ho - li - er than thou!
Bar.
thou, huh! Ho - li - er than thou!
Bs.
thou, huh! Ho - li - er than thou!
A C A G A G Em G A C A G
Pno.

59
T. I
T. II
Bar.
Bs.
Pno.
mf
Ya want us to scrape and
Ya want us to hark-en and take heed?
A
D
G
D
f
mf
64
Ho - li - er__ than thou, yes!__
bow?
yes!__
Then drop the an - gel at - ti - tude,__
yes!__
yes!__
A
A7
D
G
G7
F♯m/A

979-0-051-48498-0

69
T. I
Ho - li - er___ than thou.
T. II
Ho - li - er___ than thou.
Bar.
Ho - li - er___ than thou.
Bs.
Ho - li - er___ than thou.
G7 D G7 D G7
Pno.
74
T. I
Down here, we don't have time for that___ Ho - li - er___ than
T. II
Ho - li - er___ than
Bar.
Ho - li - er___ than
Bs.
Ho - li - er___ than
D Bm G7/D
Pno.

79
T. I
thou.
T. II
thou. If you come down to earth, come all the way, come all the
Bar.
thou. come all the
Bs.
thou. come all the
Bm G/B Bm/D
Pno.
83
T. I
not ho - li - er than thou, ho-ho - ho - li - er than thou.
T. II
way, not ho - li - er than thou, ho-ho - ho - li - er than thou.
Bar.
way, not ho - li - er than thou, ho-ho - ho - li - er than thou.
Bs.
way, not ho - li - er than thou, ho-ho - ho - li - er than thou.
E F♯ A F♯ E F♯ A F♯
Pno.

88
T. I
You got that
T. II
Bar.
Bs.
A F♯ A F♯
Pno.
f

93
T. I
an - gel at - ti - tude,___ You got that an - gel at -
T. II
Ho - li - er___ than thou. You got that an - gel at -
Bar.
Ho - li - er___ than thou.
Bs.
Ho - li - er___ than thou.
G7 Am7 D7 G7
Pno.
mf

98
T. I
ti - tude,
Make your-selves un - pop - u - lar
T. II
ti - tude, Ho - li - er than thou, oh yeah! Ah
mp
Bar.
Ho - li - er than thou, oh yeah! Ah
mp
Bs.
Ho - li - er than thou, oh yeah! Ah
mp
Pno.
Am7 D7 G7 Dm7
103
T. I
with that an - gel at - ti - tude. Ho - li - er than thou, huh! Ho - li - er than
T. II
Ho - li - er than thou, huh! Ho - li - er than
mf
Bar.
Ho - li - er than thou, huh! Ho - li - er than
mf
Bs.
Ho - li - er than thou, huh! Ho - li - er than
mf
Pno.
G7 Dm7 G A

979-0-051-48498-0

108
T. I
thou!
T. II
thou!
Bar.
thou!
Bs.
thou!
A C A G A G Em G A C A G A
Pno.
f
113
T. I
T. II
Ya want us to scrape and bow?
Bar.
Ya want us to hark-en and take heed? Then
Bs.
D G D A A7
Pno.
mf

118
T. I
T. II
Bar.
Bs.
Pno.
Ho-li - er__ than thou, yes!__ Ho-li - er__ than
drop the an-gel at - ti - tude,__
D
G
G7
F♯m/A
G7/B
123
thou.____ Ho-li - er__ than thou, yes!__ Ho-li - er__ than thou.
Ho-li - er__ than thou, yes!__ Ho-li - er__ than thou.
Ho-li - er__ than thou, yes!__ Ho-li - er__ than thou.
Ho-li - er__ than thou, yes!__ Ho-li - er__ than thou.
D
G7
D/A
G7
D

979-0-051-48498-0

979-0-051-48498-0

V. And Am I Born to Die?

SATB Choir, Gospel Quartet and Band

IDUMEA - Charles Wesley (1707-1788)

Ananias Davisson (1780-1857)
arr. Carol Barnett

BAND MEMBER #1: *But, the question remains, if we mortals think we have all the answers, then why are we here? What are we doing here on earth?*

979-0-051-48498-0

Engraved & Printed in U.S.A.

9
T. I
must my trem - bling spir - it fly In - to a world un -
Bar.
Bs.
Pno.
12
T. I
known? A land of deep - est shade, Un - pierced by hu - man
mp
Bar.
A land of deep - est shade, Un - pierced by hu - man
mp
Bs.
A land of deep - est shade, Un - pierced by hu - man
Am C Am Em G C
Pno.

979-0-051-48498-0

16
T. I
thought; The drear - y re - gions of the dead, Where
Bar.
thought; The drear - y re - gions of the dead, Where
Bs.
thought; The drear - y re - gions of the dead, Where
Em G Em Am G
Pno.
19
T. I
mf
all things are for - got. Soon as from earth I
Bar.
mf
all things are for - got. Soon as from earth I
Bs.
mf
all things are for - got. Soon as from earth I
Am C Dm Am C
Pno.
mf

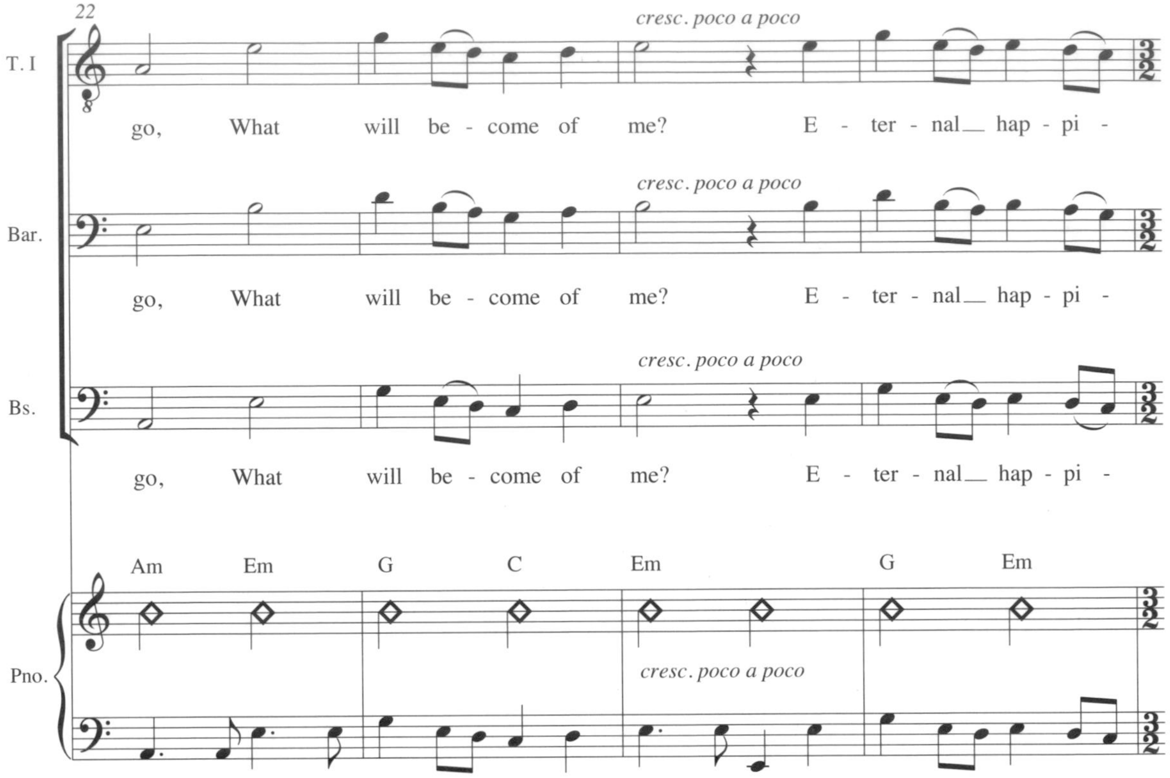
22
cresc. poco a poco
T. I
go, What will be - come of me? E - ter - nal hap - pi -
cresc. poco a poco
Bar.
go, What will be - come of me? E - ter - nal hap - pi -
cresc. poco a poco
Bs.
go, What will be - come of me? E - ter - nal hap - pi -
Am Em G C Em G Em
Pno.
cresc. poco a poco

26
T. I
ness or woe Must then my por - tion be.
Bar.
ness or woe Must then my por - tion be.
Bs.
ness or woe Must then my por - tion be.
Am G Am C Dm Em
Pno.

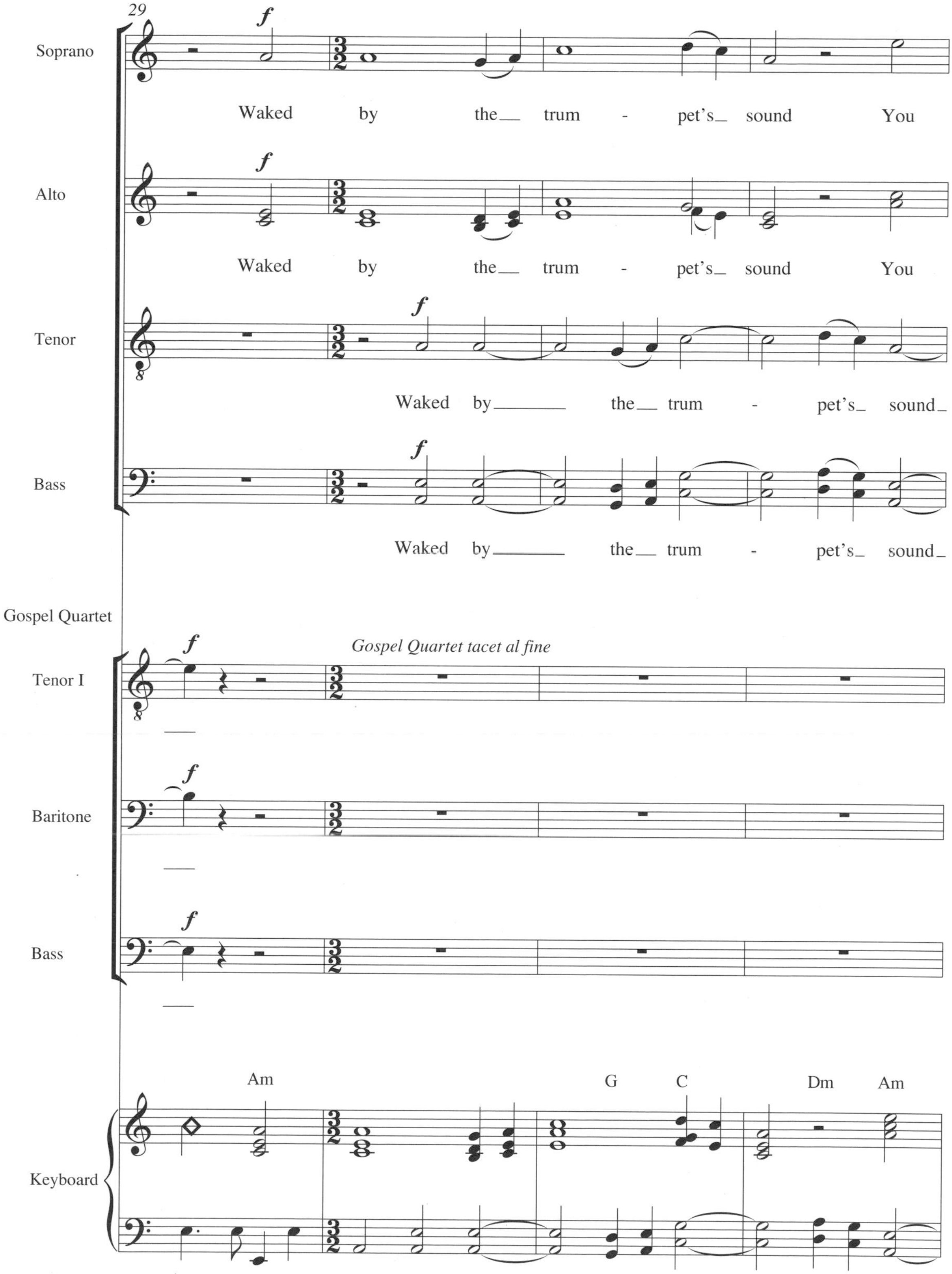
29
Soprano
Waked by the trum - pet's sound You
Alto
Waked by the trum - pet's sound You
Tenor
Waked by the trum - pet's sound
Bass
Waked by the trum - pet's sound
Gospel Quartet
Gospel Quartet tacet al fine
Tenor I
Baritone
Bass
Am
G
C
Dm
Am
Keyboard

33
cresc.
S.
from your grave shall rise,
A.
from your grave shall rise, shall
T.
You from your grave shall rise,
B.
You from your grave shall rise,
Am7 Em C/G Am/E Cmaj9 Cmaj7 Dm Em
Pno.
36
piu f
And see the Judge with glo - ry
rise, And see the Judge with glo - ry
And see the Judge with glo - ry
And see the Judge with glo - ry
Am/E Em A7 A7/G A/F Em D C

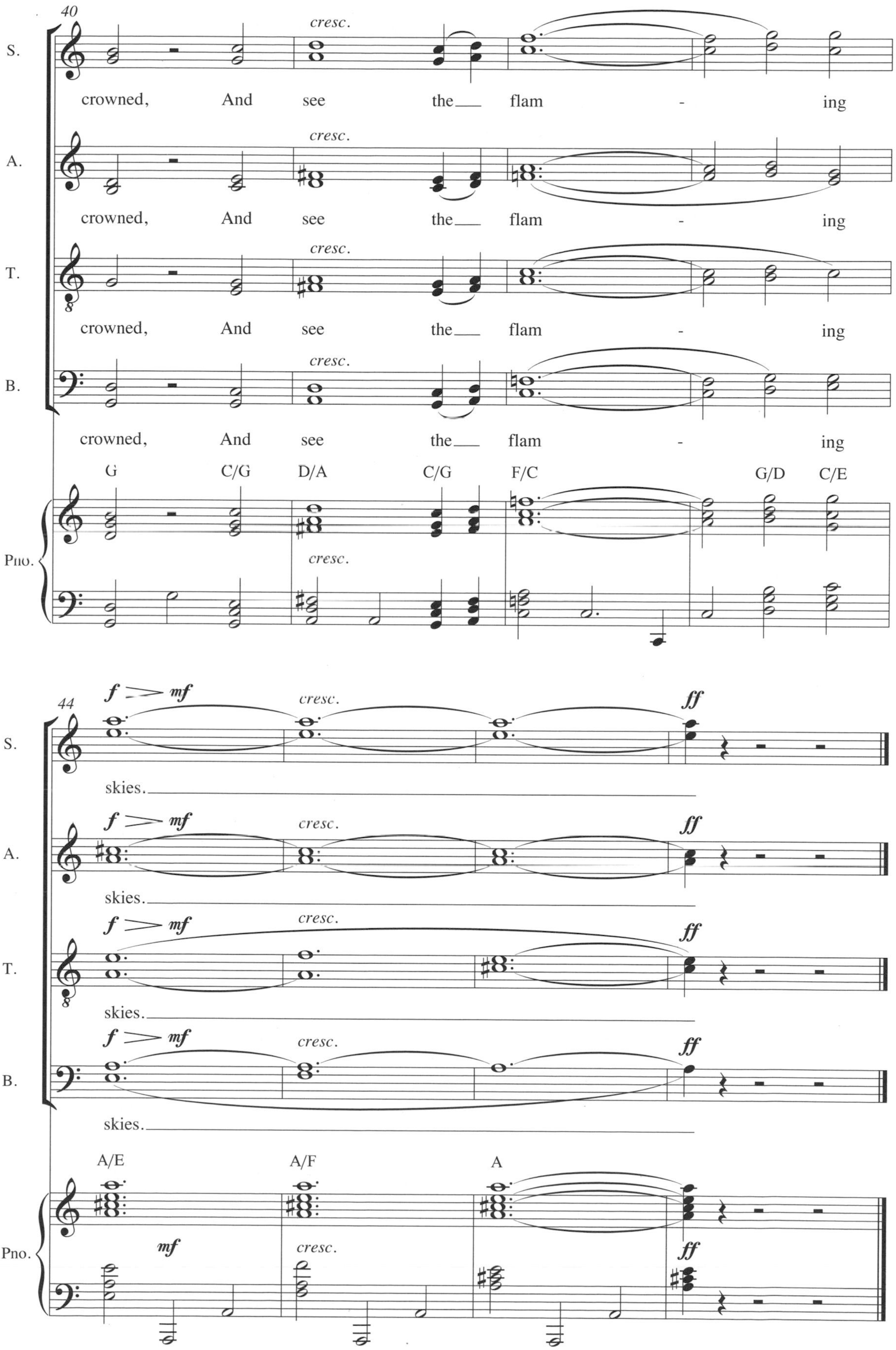

979-0-051-48498-0

VI. Bad Days Are Coming

Treble Chorus and Band

Marisha Chamberlain

Carol Barnett

Agitato 𝅗𝅥 = ca. 104
Treble Chorus
mf
We know bad days are com- ing, are com- ing.
Agitato 𝅗𝅥 = ca. 104
(Fiddle, Mandolin, Banjo, Guitar, Bass)
Gm F Gm Dm7 Gm
Keyboard
f
mf
5
T.C.
Bad days are com- ing, are com- ing. We know bad days are
Dm7 Gm Dm7
Pno.
8
T.C.
com- ing, are com- ing. Bad days, bad days. We days. The
1
2
Gm F 1 Gm 2 Gm
Pno.

979-0-051-48498-0

Engraved & Printed in U.S.A.

12
T.C.
shores start to crum - ble And the gla - ciers_ all shrink, The
C Gm7 C Gm/B♭ C Gm7 C Gm/B♭
Pno.
16
T.C.
cresc.
riv - ers_ dry up And there's noth - ing to
C Gm7 C
Pno.
cresc.
20
T.C.
f
mf
drink. We know bad days are
D C D Gm Dm7
Pno.
f
mf
23
T.C.
com-ing, are com-ing. Bad days are com-ing, are com-ing. We
Gm Dm7 Gm Gm/B♭
Pno.

26
T.C.
Pno.
know bad days are com-ing, are com-ing. Bad days, bad days.
Gm Dm7 Gm Gm/B♭ Gm F Gm
30
cresc.
f
Bad days, bad days. Bad days, bad days.
Gm F Gm Dm7 Gm7
cresc.
dim.
34
mp
And the air is all ash - es.
Am/D A♭/G Gm C B♭ C
39
cresc.
Soon noth - ing will thrive, And the cit - ies are
Gm7 Gm7/B♭ C B♭ C Dm B♭ C Gm7 C B♭

979-0-051-48498-0

T.C.
Pno.
44
burn - ing, And zom - bies ar -
C Cm Cm/A D E♭ E F D C
f
49
rive. We know bad days are com-ing, are com-ing.
D C D Gm Dm7 Gm
mf
53
Bad days are com-ing, are com-ing. We know bad days are
Dm7 Gm Dm7
56
com-ing, are com-ing. Bad days, bad days. We know bad days are
Gm F Gm Gm Dm7
p

60
T.C.
com- ing, are com- ing. Bad days are com- ing, are com- ing. We
Gm Dm7 Gm
Pno.
63
T.C.
know bad days are com- ing, are com- ing. Bad days are
Dm7 Gm Dm7
Pno.
66
cresc.
T.C.
com- ing, com- ing. Bad days are com- ing, com- ing. Bad days are
Gm7 Dm7 Gm Dm7 Gm7 Dm7 Gm7 Dm7
Pno.
cresc.
70
ff
T.C.
com- ing, com- ing. Ah
Gm7 Dm7 B♭/D Gm F Gm
Pno.
ff

BAND MEMBER # 1: *(to the treble choir)* Did I hear that right? The cities are burning and zombies arrive? Zombies? You believe in zombies?!?

BAND MEMBER #2: Well, just let me say that my kids believe in zombies.

(Angels shake their heads, disapproving.)

BAND MEMBER #1: *(to the angels)* No to zombies? Or is it no to any jokes at all? Well, be that as it may…

VII. We Don't Stay Afraid for Long

Gospel Quartet and Band

Marisha Chamberlain

Jamie Dailey
Carol Barnett

979-0-051-48498-0

Engraved & Printed in U.S.A.

7
T. I
Hell to pay, but you know us, We don't stay a - fraid for long.
T. II
Bar.
Bs.
C Bm/D C Em C D
Pno.
10
T. I
God help us, we don't stay a-fraid for long. God
T. II
mp
God
Bar.
mp
God
Bs.
mp
God
Em C Em/B Am7 Bm/D D7 G
Pno.

14
T. I
T. II
Bar.
Bs.
Pno.
help us, we don't stay a-fraid_ for__ long.
(+ Fiddle & Mandolin)
C6 Em7/B Am7 Bm/D D7 G Am7/G
18
Fright-en us__ with the wrath of God,_ But we
(– Fiddle, Mandolin & Banjo)
G Am7/D G

22
T. I
nev-er stay fright-ened long.
Hell to pay, but you know us,
T. II
nev-er stay fright-ened long.
Hell to pay, but you know us,
Bar.
Bs.
Am C/D Bm/D G C Bm/D C Em
Pno.
26
T. I
we don't stay a - fraid for long.
God help us, we don't
T. II
we don't stay a - fraid for long.
God help us, we don't
Bar.
Bs.
C D Em C Em/B
Pno.

979-0-051-48498-0

29
T. I
stay a-fraid_ for_ long. God help us, we don't stay a-fraid_ for_
T. II
stay a-fraid_ for_ long. God help us, we don't stay a-fraid_ for_
Bar.
God help us, we don't stay a-fraid_ for_
Bs.
God help us, we don't stay a-fraid_ for_
Am7 Bm/D D7 G C6 Em7/B Am7 Bm/D D7
Pno.
33
long.
long.
Oh,
mf
long.
long.
(+ Fiddle, Mandolin & Banjo)
G Am7/G G Am7/D
mf

37
T. I
T. II
some of us be-lieve in zom - bies, Some, in fair-ies and elves.
Bar.
Bs.
(– Fiddle, Mandolin & Banjo)
Em Am Em Am/C D
mp
Pno.
41
T. I
T. II
Some of us be-lieve in an - gels, And some of us just be - lieve
Bar.
Bs.
G G/B Em Em7/D Am/C
Pno.

979-0-051-48498-0

52
T. I
wrath of God, but we nev - er stay fright - ened long.
T. II
wrath of God, but we nev - er stay fright - ened long.
Bar.
Bs.
Am C/D Bm/D G
Pno.
55
T. I
Hell to pay, but you know us, We don't stay a - fraid for long.
T. II
Hell to pay, but you know us, We don't stay a - fraid for long.
Bar.
Bs.
C Bm/D C Em C D Em
Pno.

979-0-051-48498-0

58
T. I
T. II
Bar.
Bs.
Pno.
God help us, we don't stay a-fraid_ for_ long.
mp
(+Fiddle, Mandolin & Banjo)
C6 Em7/B Am7 Bm/D D7 G
mf
62
We may not have the sense That God gave geese. We
Gmaj7 G6
(—Fiddle, Mandolin, Banjo)
C C7 C
mp

65
T. I
T. II
Bar.
don't have the wings_ of an - gels. But Lord_ Al-might - y, We
Bs.
G
C
Pno.
68
T. I
T. II
Bar.
do have nerve, And we don't stay a - fraid_ for long.__
Bs.
(+Fiddle, Mandolin & Banjo)
G
A7
Am7/D
mf
Pno.

979-0-051-48498-0

71
T. I
T. II
Bar.
Bs.
mp
Fright-en us with the wrath of God, But we
Pno.
D7
G
p
74
nev - er stay fright - ened long.
Hell to pay, but
Am
D
Em
C

77
T. I
T. II
Bar.
Bs.
you know us, We don't stay a - fraid for long.___ God
Em C Em D Em
Pno.
80
T. I
T. II
Bar.
Bs.
help us, we don't stay a - fraid_ for_ long.
(+ Mandolin)
C Em7 Em/B D7 G
mf
Pno.

84
T. I
T. II
Bar.
Bs.
Pno.
mf
Hell to pay, but you know us, We don't stay a - fraid for long. God
Cmaj7 D7 Cmaj7 Em Am7 Cmaj7 D Em
88
help us, we don't stay a-fraid for long. God help us, we don't
mp
Am7/C Em7/B Am7 Bm/D D7 G Am7/C Em7/B

92
T. I
stay a-fraid_ for_ long. God help us, we don't stay a-fraid___
T. II
stay a-fraid_ for_ long. God help us, we don't stay a-fraid___
Bar.
stay a-fraid_ for_ long. God help us, we don't stay a-fraid___
Bs.
stay a-fraid_ for_ long. God help us, we don't stay a-fraid___
p
Am7 Bm/D D7 Em Em/D Am7/C Em7/B Am7 Bm/D
Pno.
96
T. I
__ for long.___
T. II
__ for long.___
Bar.
__ for long.___
Bs.
__ for long.___
D7 G
Pno.

(Archangel steps down to the Band and puts his arms around two of the Band members.)

BAND: Oh my! An Angel? So are you joining us, too? Going to be one of the Mortals?

ARCHANGEL: *(takes a step backward, shakes his head and raises his hands)* No, I'm not joining you.

VIII. Down to the River

Baritone Solo, SATB Choir and Band

Marisha Chamberlain
adapted from a poem by Lisel Mueller

Carol Barnett

Cantabile ♩ = ca. 112
Baritone Solo
Keyboard
(Mandolin, Banjo, Guitar, Bass)
(—Mandolin, Banjo)
Dmaj7 Em/A Dmaj7 Em/A D
mp
p
The sun drapes the riv-er with a shiv-er of light.
The chil-dren come down to be healed.
The fa-thers who gave them their wounds and their bruis - es come to be healed of their rage.
The
Bar. Solo
Pno.
Bm A/C♯ F♯m G
D Em A D Bm A/C♯
F♯m Em7 Em/C♯ F♯ F♯7
mf

979-0-051-48498-0

Engraved & Printed in U.S.A.

22
Bar. Solo
moth - ers grow love - ly; their fac - es sof - ten, The
Bm F♯m Em A D
mp
Pno.
28
Bar. Solo
birds in their throats a - wake. They stand hand in hand and the
Em7 A7 D C G
Pno.
34
Bar. Solo
trees a - round lean o - ver them, sing - ing of heav - en,
dim.
Em Bm Em A9 Dmaj7
(Fiddle, Mandolin & Banjo)
Pno.
40
Bar. Solo
heav - en, heav - en.
p
Gmaj9 Bm9 Em7 A
p
Pno.

46
Bar. Solo
(Band improv.)
D
Bm
A/C♯
F♯m
F♯m7
G
mf
Pno.
52
Bar. Solo
D
Em7
A
D
Bm
Pno.
58
Bar. Solo
F♯m
Em
Em/C♯
F♯
F♯7
Bm
F♯m
Pno.
65
Bar. Solo
Em
A
D
Em7
A7
D
Pno.

72
Bar. Solo
Pno.
C G Em Bm Em
78
Bar. Solo
Pno.
A9 Dmaj7 Gmaj9 Bm9
84
Soprano
S.
pp stagger breathing
Oo
Alto
A.
pp stagger breathing
Oo
Tenor
T.
mp
The sun drapes the riv-er with a shiv-er of
Bass
B.
mp
The sun drapes the riv-er with a shiv-er of
Pno.
Em7 A D F♯m
mp

90
S.
A.
T.
light. The chil-dren come down to be healed. The
B.
light. The chil-dren come down to be healed. The
F♯m7 G D Em A
Pno.
96
S.
A.
T.
fa-thers who gave them their wounds and their bruis - es come to be
B.
fa-thers who gave them their wounds and their bruis - es come to be
D Bm A/C♯ F♯m Em
Pno.

101
cresc.
p
mf
healed of their rage. The moth - ers grow love - ly;
Em/C♯ F♯ F♯7 Bm F♯m
106
their fac - es soft - en, The birds in their throats a -
Em A D Em7 A7
S.
A.
T.
B.
Pno.

979-0-051-48498-0

112
S.
A.
T.
wake. They stand hand in hand and the trees a-round lean
B.
wake. They stand hand in hand and the trees a-round lean
D C G Em Bm
Pno.
118
dim.
S.
dim.
A.
dim.
T.
o - ver them, sing-ing of heav-en, heav-en,
dim.
B.
o - ver them, sing-ing of heav-en, heav-en,
Em G/A A7 Dmaj7 Gmaj9
Pno.
dim.

979-0-051-48498-0

BAND MEMBER #1: Well, that's… very mystical. But we're not done arguing. We mortals will never be done arguing and wrestling with angels.

IX. Jacob Wrestled With the Angel

Baritone Solo, Gospel Quartet and Band

Marisha Chamberlain

Carol Barnett

Animato ♩ = ca. 100
Baritone Solo
Keyboard
mf
A
mp
Ja-cob's peo-ple crossed the riv-er While
5
Bar. Solo
Pno.
Ja-cob stayed on a - lone, And caught him an an-gel, laid hold of an an-gel, Though
E
A
9
Ja-cob was fright-ened to the bone, was fright-ened to the bone.
E
A
D
E

979-0-051-48498-0

Engraved & Printed in U.S.A.

13
Bar. Solo
T. I
T. II
Bar.
Bs.
Pno.
mf
Oh, Ja - cob wres-tled that an-gel; They wres-tled till the break of
A
D A
17
day. "I won't let you go till you bless me," said Ja - cob, Though the
day. "I won't let you go till you bless me," said Ja - cob,
E
A
D
A
D A

979-0-051-48498-0

21
Bar. Solo
an-gel tried to get a-way, he tried to get a - way.
dim.
T. I
an-gel tried to get a-way, he tried to get a - way.
dim.
T. II
he tried to get a - way.
dim.
Bar.
he tried to get a - way.
dim.
Bs.
he tried to get a - way.
dim.
E A E7 A
Pno.
dim.
27
mf
The an-gel nev-er tir-ed for a min-ute, Though he want-ed to be
mp

31
Bar. Solo
gone. "I won't let you go till you bless me," said Ja-cob, So the two of them wres-tled
T. I
T. II
Bar.
Bs.
E A D A D A
Pno.
36
Bar. Solo
on and on, the two of them wres-tled on.
T. I
T. II
Bar.
Bs.
E A D E
Pno.

979-0-051-48498-0

40
Bar. Solo
Oh, Ja - cob wres-tled that an-gel; They wres-tled till the break of
T. I
mf
Oh, Ja - cob wres-tled that an-gel; They wres-tled till the break of
T. II
mf
Oh, Ja - cob wres-tled that an-gel; They wres-tled till the break of
Bar.
mf
Oh, Ja - cob wres-tled that an-gel; They wres-tled till the break of
Bs.
mf
Oh, Ja - cob wres-tled that an-gel; They wres-tled till the break of
A D A
Pno.
mf
44
Bar. Solo
day. "I won't let you go till you bless me," said Ja-cob, Though the an-gel tried to
T. I
day. "I won't let you go till you bless me," said Ja-cob, Though the an-gel tried to
T. II
day. "I won't let you go till you bless me," said Ja-cob,
Bar.
day. "I won't let you go till you bless me," said Ja-cob,
Bs.
day. "I won't let you go till you bless me," said Ja-cob,
E A D A D A
Pno.

49
Bar. Solo
get a-way, he tried to get a - way.
dim.
T. I
get a-way, he tried to get a - way.
dim.
T. II
he tried to get a - way.
dim.
Bar.
he tried to get a - way.
dim.
Bs.
he tried to get a - way.
dim.
E A E7 A
Pno.
dim.

55
mf
Bar. Solo
Ja-cob got a cramp in his el-bow, In his knee, in his shoul-der, in his
T. I
T. II
Bar.
Bs.
Pno.
mp

59
Bar. Solo
knee, in his shoul-der, in his hip. "Let's shake hands and go,"_ the an-gel said, But
T. I
T. II
Bar.
Bs.
E
A
D
A
Pno.
65
Bar. Solo
Ja-cob was too stub-born to quit, he was too stub-born to quit.
T. I
T. II
Bar.
Bs.
E
A
D
E
Pno.
cresc.

979-0-051-48498-0

70
Bar. Solo
T. I
T. II
Bar.
Bs.
Pno.
mf
Oh, Ja - cob wres-tled that an-gel; They wres-tled till the break of
A
D A
74
day. "I won't let you go till you bless me," said Ja - cob, Though the
day. "I won't let you go till you bless me," said Ja - cob,
E
A
D
A
D A

78
Bar. Solo
T. I
T. II
Bar.
Bs.
Pno.
dim.
an - gel tried to get a - way, he tried to get a - way.
he tried to get a - way.
E A E7 A
83
mf
mp
“O - kay,” said the an - gel “I’ll bless you, ’Cuz it
E A

87
Bar. Solo
looks like you're in pain. O - kay,"said the an-gel,_"I'll bless you,_ But first I got-ta
T. I
T. II
Bar.
Bs.
E
A
Pno.
92
Bar. Solo
know your name,_ I got-ta know your name."_
T. I
T. II
Bar.
Bs.
E
A
D
E
Pno.

979-0-051-48498-0

96
Bar. Solo
Oh, Ja - cob wres-tled that an-gel; They wres-tled till the break of day. "I...
T. I
mf
Oh, Ja - cob wres-tled that an-gel; They wres-tled till the break of day. "I
T. II
mf
Oh, Ja - cob wres-tled that an-gel; They wres-tled till the break of day. "I
Bar.
mf
Oh, Ja - cob wres-tled that an-gel; They wres-tled till the break of day. "I
Bs.
mf
Oh, Ja - cob wres-tled that an-gel; They wres-tled till the break of day. "I
A
D A
E
Pno.
mf

(Singing halts, mid-chorus.)

CONDUCTOR: *(To the audience)* So, Jacob wrestled with the angel, and wouldn't quit, wouldn't let the angel go until he got a blessing. And the angel said, "I'll bless you. What is your name?" *(Addressing a band member:)* What is your name?

(Band member says her name.)

CONDUCTOR: *(Addressing all band members)* And your name? And yours?

(They speak their names.)

CONDUCTOR: Angels, do these Mortals have your blessing?

ANGELS: Yes.

BAND: Wait, we'd like to get in on this, too. May we, the mere Mortals, give our blessings, too? What's your name? Blessings. Say, Conductor, this could take all night. How about everybody bless each other by saying our names together.

(The Conductor directs the audience, choir and band to speak their names together.)

(The Quartet starts up again just as suddenly as it stopped.)

101
L'istesso
mf
Bar. Solo
T. I
T. II
Bar.
Bs.
Oh, Ja - cob wres-tled that an-gel; They wres-tled till the break of
L'istesso
A
D A
Pno.
106
day. "I won't let you go till you bless me," said Ja-cob, Though the an-gel tried to
day. "I won't let you go till you bless me," said Ja-cob,
E
A
D
A
D A

979-0-051-48498-0

111
Bar. Solo
T. I
T. II
Bar.
Bs.
Pno.
cresc.
get a - way, he tried to get a - way, he tried to get a - way, he
he tried to get a - way, he tried to get a - way, he
E A E7 F#m Bm7/D A G#dim F#m Bm7/D
116
f
tried to get a - way.
A/E Bm7/E E7 A

X. Ev'ry Step to Heaven is Heaven

SATB Choir and Band

Marisha Chamberlain

Carol Barnett

BAND MEMBER #2: Okay, so if there's a better land waiting by and by, where would it be? We don't know. … Could it be right here? Like, where we are already? With these people around us? And with these angels?

979-0-051-48498-0

Engraved & Printed in U.S.A.

9
S.
A.
T.
B.
Ev - 'ry step_ to heav-en is heav-en, heav-en, heav-en, heav-en, heav-en.
heav-en, heav-en.
D
D6
Pno.
13
mf
Ev-'ry step to heav-en is heav-en.
D6/A
D
mf
mp

17
S.
Ev - 'ry step _ to heav-en is heav-en,
A.
mf
Ev-'ry step to heav-en is heav-en it-self. _
T.
B.
A7
D
A7
D
Pno.
21
S.
heav-en, heav-en, heav-en, heav-en.
A.
heav-en, heav-en, heav-en, heav-en.
T.
B.
D6
D6/A
D6
D6/A
mf
Pno.

25
S.
A.
T.
B.
p
Through the val-ley of shad - ow,
Through the val-ley of light,
Em7
Em7/A
A7
D
Pno.
p
29
mp
Through the val-ley of shad - ow,
cresc.
Through the val-ley of light,
mf
light,
mf
light,
Am7
D7
G
Em7
A
mp
cresc.

33
S.
A.
T.
B.
Pno.
mf
Ev-'ry step to heav-en is heav-en.
mf
Ev-'ry step to heav-en is heav-en. Ev-'ry step to heav-en is heav-en it - self._
light.
Ev-'ry step to heav-en is heav-en it - self._
light.
D
Em7
Em7/A
D
A
mf
mp
37
S.
A.
T.
B.
Pno.
Ev-'ry step to heav-en is heav-en, heav-en, heav-en,
Ev-'ry step to heav-en is heav-en, heav-en, heav-en,
Ev-'ry step to heav-en is heav-en, heav-en, heav-en,
heav-en, heav-en,
D
D6
D6/A

41
S.
A.
T.
B.
heav-en, heav-en, heav-en, ah.
heav-en, heav-en, heav-en, ah.
heav-en, heav-en, heav-en, ah.
heav-en, heav-en, heav-en, ah.
p
D6 Bm7 Bm D7/A D7 G
(opt. improv.)
Pno.
p sub. mf
45
S.
A.
T.
B.
D G D G
Pno.

49
S.
A.
T.
B.
G6
C Am/E
G Em
G
Em7
Pno.
53
mp
Through the val-ley of laugh - ter,
Through the val-ley of tears,
mp
Through the val-ley of laugh - ter,
Through the val-ley of tears,
mp
Through the val-ley of tears,
A7
D
p

57
S.
A.
T.
B.
Pno.
ah.
ah.
Through the val-ley of laugh - ter,
Through the val-ley of tears,
ah.
mp
Through the val-ley of laugh - ter,
Through the val-ley of tears,
ah.
Am
D7
G
Em7
A
61
p
mp
Ev-'ry step to heav-en is heav-en, heav-en, heav-en, heav-en, heav-en,
heav-en, heav-en,
D
D6
G
D6
G

979-0-051-48498-0

65
S.
ah.
A.
ah.
T.
mp
heav-en, heav-en, heav-en, heav-en.
p
Through the val-ley of shad-
B.
mp
heav-en, heav-en.
p
Through the val-ley of shad-
D6 Em7 D6 Em7 A7
Pno.
pp
68
S.
p
Through the val-ley of shad - ow,
cresc.
Through the val-ley of light,
A.
p
Through the val-ley of shad - ow,
cresc.
Through the val-ley of light,
T.
- ow,
Through the val-ley of light,
cresc.
B.
- ow,
Through the val-ley of light,
cresc.
D
Pno.
p

71
S.
A.
T.
B.
Pno.
mp
Through the val-ley of laugh - ter,
Through the val-ley of laugh - ter,
Through the val-ley of laugh - ter,
Through the val-ley of tears,
Through the val-ley of laugh - ter,
Through the val-ley of tears,
A7
D
74
mf
Through the val-ley of tears,
Through the val-ley of shad - ow,
Through the val-ley of tears,
Through the val-ley of shad - ow,
Through the val-ley of shad - ow,
Through the val-ley of shad - ow,
D7

77
S.
A.
T.
B.
Pno.
f
p
cresc. poco a poco
light, laugh - ter and tears.
Ev-'ry step is heav-en,
D7/C G D Em7 D/A D6/A
81
Ev-'ry step is heav-en, heav-en, heav-en,
D/A Em/A D/A Em/A

85
f
S.
heav - en,
ah,
A.
T.
B.
Pno.
89
dim.
mf
ah.

XI. Angels Hov'ring 'Round

Tenor Solo, SATB Choir, Treble Chorus and Band

Traditional
adapted by Marisha Chamberlain

Traditional
arranged by Carol Barnett

Marziale ♩ = ca. 120
Tenor Solo
Keyboard
G Em G
f
Oh, there are an - gels, an - gels hov - 'ring
Tenor Solo
'round, hov - 'ring 'round.
Treble Chorus
Soprano Alto
Tenor I, II
f
mf
hov - 'ring 'round. There are an - gels hov - 'ring 'round, There are
Baritone Bass
hov - 'ring 'round. There are an - gels hov - 'ring 'round, There are
Keyboard
D D7 C G
mf

979-0-051-48498-0

Engraved & Printed in U.S.A.

9
T. Solo
Treble Chorus
S. A.
T. I, II
an - gels hov - 'ring 'round, There are an - gels, an - gels
Bar. Bs.
an - gels hov - 'ring 'round, There are an - gels, an - gels
Am7/D D G D G Am/C
Kbd.
13
T. Solo
Treble Chorus
mf
There are an - gels hov - 'ring 'round, There are
S. A.
mf
There are an - gels hov - 'ring 'round, There are
T. I, II
hov - 'ring 'round. There are an - gels hov - 'ring 'round, There are
Bar. Bs.
hov - 'ring 'round. There are an - gels hov - 'ring 'round, There are
G/D D7 G D C G
Kbd.
mf

979-0-051-48498-0

17
T. Solo
Treble Chorus
an - gels hov - 'ring 'round, There are an - gels,
S. A.
an - gels hov - 'ring 'round, There are an - gels,
T. I, II
an - gels hov - 'ring 'round, There are an - gels,
Bar. Bs.
an - gels hov - 'ring 'round, There are an - gels,
Am7/D D G D
Kbd.
20
T. Solo
f
There are an - gels
Treble Chorus
an - gels hov - 'ring 'round.
S. A.
an - gels hov - 'ring 'round.
T. I, II
an - gels hov - 'ring 'round.
Bar. Bs.
an - gels hov - 'ring 'round.
G Am/C G/D D7 G
Kbd.
f

24
T. Solo
hov - 'ring 'round To car - ry the ti - dings home.
Treble Chorus
mf
To car - ry the ti - dings
S. A.
mf
To car - ry the ti - dings
T. I, II
mf
To car - ry the ti - dings
Bar. Bs.
mf
To car - ry the ti - dings,
C/D D7
Kbd.
28
T. Solo
Treble Chorus
home, To car - ry the ti - dings home, To
S. A.
home, To car - ry the ti - dings home, To
T. I, II
home, To car - ry the ti - dings home, To
home, To car - ry the ti - dings home, To
Bar. Bs.
f mf f mf
ti - dings home, To car - ry the ti - dings, ti - dings home, To
G D
Kbd.
mf

979-0-051-48498-0

T. Solo
Treble Chorus
S. A.
T. I, II
Bar. Bs.
Kbd.
car - ry, car - ry the ti - dings home.
To
G D Am/C G/D D7 G
car - ry the ti - dings home To the New Je - ru - sa - lem.
To the
G C G Am7/D D

39
T. Solo
Treble Chorus
New Je - ru - sa - lem, To the New Je - ru - sa - lem, To the
S.
New Je - ru - sa - lem, To the New Je - ru - sa - lem, To the
A.
New Je - ru - sa - lem, To the New Je - ru - sa - lem, To the
T. I
New Je - ru - sa - lem, To the New Je - ru - sa - lem, To the
T. II
New Je - ru - sa - lem, To the New Je - ru - sa - lem, To the
Bar.
New Je - ru - sa - lem, To the New Je - ru - sa - lem, To the
Bs.
f mf f mf
New Je - ru - sa - lem, Je-ru - sa- lem, To the New Je - ru - sa - lem, Je-ru - sa- lem, To the
G D
mf
Kbd.

43
T. Solo
f
Let all, let
Treble Chorus
New, the New Je - ru - sa - lem.
S.
New, the New Je - ru - sa - lem.
A.
New, the New Je - ru - sa - lem.
T. I
f
New, the New Je - ru - sa - lem. Let all,
T. II
f
New, the New Je - ru - sa - lem. Let all,
Bar.
f
New, the New Je - ru - sa - lem. Let all,
Bs.
f
New, the New Je - ru - sa - lem. Let all,
G D G Am/C G/D D7 G C G
Kbd.
f

48
Tenor Solo tacet al fine
T. Solo
all, let all that hear them come.
Treble Chorus
mf
Let all that hear them come, Let
S. I
mf
Let all that hear them come, Let
S. II
mf
Let all that hear them come, Let
A.
mf
Let all that hear them come, Let
T. I
let all, let all that hear them come.
mf
Let all that hear them come, Let
T. II
let all, let all that hear them come.
mf
Let all that hear them, come, Let
Bar.
let all, let all that hear them come.
mf
Let all that hear them, come, Let
Bs.
let all, let all that hear them come.
mf
Let all that hear them,
f
hear them come,
mf
Let
Am/C G
D
G
Kbd.
mf

979-0-051-48498-0

53
Treble Chorus
all that hear them come,___ Let all___ let all___ that_ hear them
S. I
all that hear them come,___ Let all___ let all___ that hear them
S. II
all that hear them come,___ Let all___ let all___ that_ hear them
A.
all that hear them come,___ Let all___ let all___ that hear them
T. I
all that hear them come,___ Let all,___ let all___ that hear them
T. II
all that hear them come,___ Let all,___ let all___ that_ hear them
Bar.
all that hear them come,___ Let all,___ let all___ that hear them
Bs.
f mf
all that hear them, hear them come, Let all,___ let all___ that hear them
Kbd.
D G D G Am/C G/D D7

58
Treble Chorus
mf
come.
There are
S. I
f
come. An - gels, an - gels hov - 'ring 'round, 'round, 'round!
There are
S. II
come. An - gels, an - gels hov - 'ring 'round, 'round, 'round!
A.
come. An - gels, an - gels hov - 'ring 'round, 'round, 'round!
T. I
come.
An - gels hov - 'ring 'round.
T. II
Bar.
Bs.
Kbd.
G
Em
D

62
Treble Chorus
an - gels hov-'ring 'round, There are an - gels hov-'ring 'round, There are
S. I
an - gels hov-'ring 'round, There are an - gels hov-'ring 'round, There are
S. II
an - gels hov-'ring 'round, There are an - gels hov-'ring 'round, There are
A. I
an - gels hov-'ring 'round, There are an - gels hov-'ring 'round, There are
A. II
an - gels hov-'ring 'round, There are an - gels hov-'ring 'round, There are
T. I
an - gels hov-'ring 'round, There are an - gels hov-'ring 'round, There are
T. II
an - gels hov-'ring 'round, There are an - gels hov-'ring 'round, There are
Bar.
an - gels hov-'ring 'round, There are an - gels hov-'ring 'round, There are
Bs.
an - gels hov-'ring, hov-'ring 'round, There are an - gels hov-'ring, hov-'ring 'round, There are
G
D
Kbd.
mf / f

66
1
f
Treble Chorus
an - gels, an - gels_ hov - 'ring 'round. There are
S. I
an - gels, an - gels hov - 'ring 'round. There are
S. II
an - gels, an - gels_ hov - 'ring 'round. There are
A. I
an - gels, an - gels hov - 'ring 'round. There are
A. II
an - gels, an - gels hov - 'ring 'round. There are
T. I
an - gels, an - gels hov - 'ring 'round. There are
T. II
an - gels, an - gels_ hov - 'ring 'round. There are
Bar.
an - gels, an - gels hov - 'ring 'round. There are
Bs.
an - gels, an - gels hov - 'ring 'round. There are
Kbd.
G D Am/C G/D D7 G D

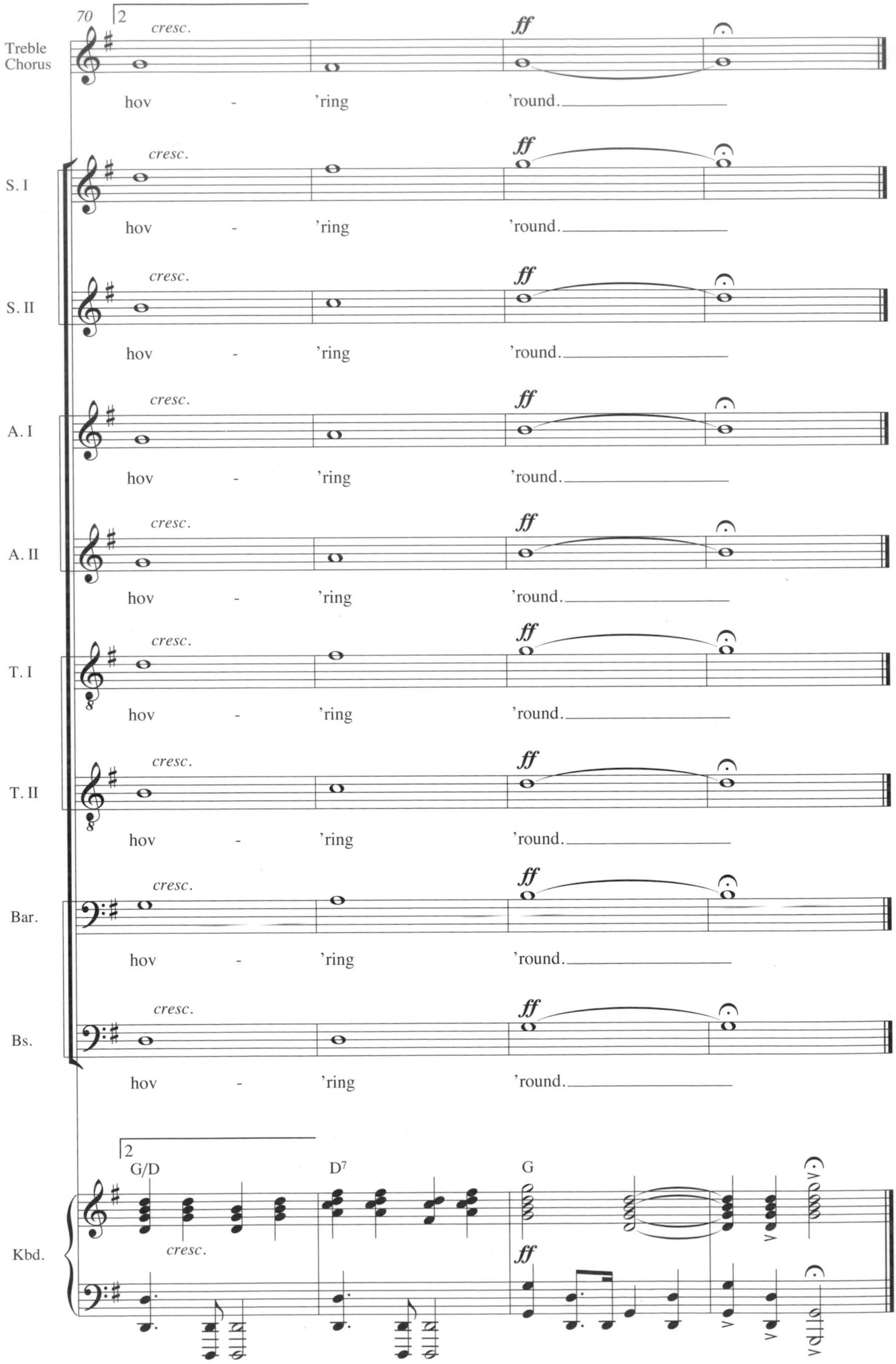

979-0-051-48498-0

XII. Angel Band

SATB Choir, Gospel Quartet, Treble Chorus and Band

Jefferson Hascall (1860)
adapted by Marisha Chamberlain

William Bradbury (1862)
Arranged by Carol Barnett

979-0-051-48498-0

Engraved & Printed in U.S.A.

9
S.
A.
T.
trou - bles of the day are past, T'ward sleep I gent - ly turn.
B.
C
F
C/G
G7
C
Kbd.

13
Tutti - add Gospel Quartet
S.
A.
mf
T.
O come, an - gel band, Come and a - round me stand; O
mf
B.
O come, an - gel band, Come and a - round me stand; O
G
C
G
C
Kbd.
mf

17
S.
A.
T.
B.
bear me a-way on your snow - y wings To my e-ter-nal home; O
bear me a-way on your snow - y wings To my e-ter-nal home; O
F C Am Dm/F E 3 E7
Kbd.
21
S.
A.
T.
B.
bear me a-way on your snow - y wings To my e - ter - nal
bear me a-way on your snow - y wings To my e - ter - nal
F C C/G Em/G Dm/G
Kbd.

24
S.
A.
T.
B.
Kbd.
pp
Oo
mp
I know I'm near the ho - ly ranks Of
home.
C
C/E
F
3
mp
28
friends and kin - dred dear. I brush the dew on Jor - dan's banks; The
G7

32
Treble Choir
S.
A.
T.
B.
Kbd.
mf
O come, an - gel band,
cross - ing may be near.
O come, an - gel band,
O come, an - gel band,
C/G Em/G G C G C
36
Come and a - round me stand; O bear me a - way on your snow - y wings To
G C F C

40
Treble Choir
my e - ter - nal home; O bear me a - way on your
S.
A.
T.
my e - ter - nal home; O bear me a - way on your
B.
my e - ter - nal home; O bear me a - way on your
Am Dm/F E E7 F
3
Kbd.
43
Treble Choir
mp
snow - y wings To my e - ter - nal home. When
S.
A.
T.
snow - y wings To my e - ter - nal home.
B.
snow - y wings To my e - ter - nal home.
C C/G Em/G Dm/G C
3
3
Kbd.

47
Treble Choir
e'er I turn to God a-bove, My spir-it loud-ly sings. The
S.
pp
Ah, my spir-it
A.
pp
Ah, my spir-it
T.
pp
Ah
B.
F/C C G7/C C
Kbd.
p
51
Conductor invites audience to join
Treble Choir
ho-ly ones, be-hold they come; I hear the noise of wings.
S.
sings. Ah Ah
A.
sings. Ah Ah
T.
B.
F/C C/G Em/G Dm/G C
Kbd.
cresc.

55
Treble Choir
S.
A.
T.
B.
Kbd.
mf
O come, angel band, Come and around me stand; O
O come, an - gel band, Come and a - round me stand; O
O come, an - gel band, Come and a - round me stand; O
G C G C
59
bear me a-way on your snow - y wings To my e - ter - nal home; O
F C Am Dm/F E E7/G♯
3

63
Treble Choir
bear me a - way on your snow - y wings To my e - ter - nal
S.
bear me a - way on your snow - y wings To my e - ter - nal
A.
bear me a - way on your snow - y wings To my e - ter - nal
T.
bear me a - way on your snow - y wings To my e - ter - nal
B.
bear me a - way on your snow - y wings To my e - ter - nal
F C C/G Em/G Dm/G
Kbd.
66
Treble Choir
f
home. O come, an - gel band, come and a -
S.
f
home. O come, an - gel band, O come and a -
A.
f
home. O come, an - gel band, O come and a -
T.
f
home. O come, an - gel band, O come and a -
B.
f
home. O come, an - gel band, come and a -
C G C G
Kbd.
f

70
Treble Choir
round me stand; O bear me a-way on your snow - y wings To my e-ter - nal
S.
round me stand; O bear me a-way on your snow - y wings To my e-ter - nal
A.
round me stand; O bear me a-way on your snow - y wings To my e-ter - nal
T.
round me stand; O bear me a-way on your snow - y wings To my e-ter - nal
B.
round me stand; O bear me a-way on your snow - y wings To my e-ter - nal
C F C Am Dm/F
Kbd.
74
Treble Choir
home. O bear me a - way on your snow - y wings To
S.
home. O bear me a - way on your snow - y wings To
A.
home. O bear me a - way on your snow - y wings To
T.
home. O bear me a - way on your snow - y wings To
B.
home. O bear me a - way on your snow - y wings To
E E7/G♯ F C
3
Kbd.

77
Treble Choir
my e - ter - nal home, To my e - ter - nal home, To
S.
my e - ter - nal home, To my e - ter - nal home, To
A.
my e - ter - nal home, To my e - ter - nal home, To
T.
my e - ter - nal home, To my e - ter - nal home, To
B.
my e - ter - nal home, To my e - ter - nal home, To
C/G Em/G Dm/G C C/G Em/G Dm/G Am F6
Kbd.
81
Treble Choir
my e - ter - nal home.
S.
my e - ter - nal home.
A.
my e - ter - nal home.
T.
my e - ter - nal home.
B.
my e - ter - nal home.
C/G Em/G Dm/G C
Kbd.
3
3
3

979-0-051-48498-0